THE BEST OF
Steven Curtis Chapman

P9-DXQ-746

Photo by Kristin G. Barlowe
Arranged by Marcel Robinson

ISBN 0-7935-9989-X

HAL•LEONARD®
CORPORATION
7777 W. BLUEMOUND RD. P.O. BOX 13819 MILWAUKEE, WI 53213

Visit Hal Leonard Online at
www.halleonard.com

THE BEST OF
Steven Curtis Chapman

For the Sake of the Call

Words and Music by Steven Curtis Chapman

We will a ban don it all for the

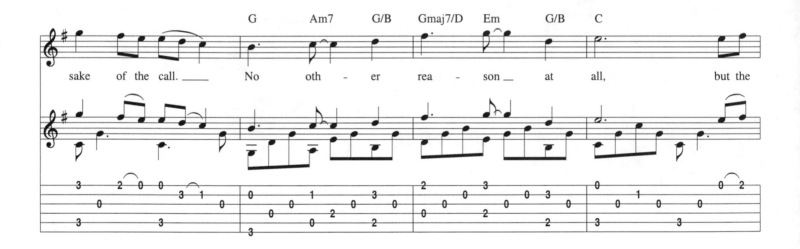

sake of the call. No oth - er rea - son at all, but the

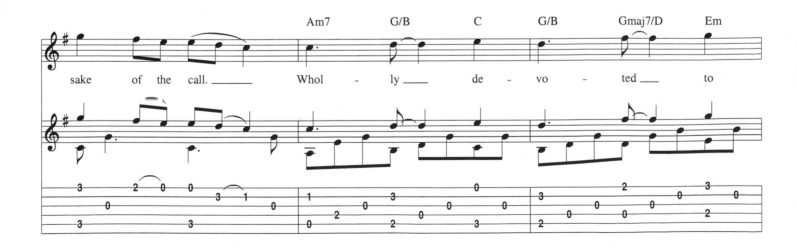

sake of the call. Whol - ly de - vo - ted to

live   and   to   die   for   the   sake   of ___ the   call.

1. No - bod - y stood   and ap - plaud - ed them, _   so they knew   from the start
2., 3. *See Additional Lyrics*

this   road would not   lead   to   fame. _____   All they   real - ly   knew _ for

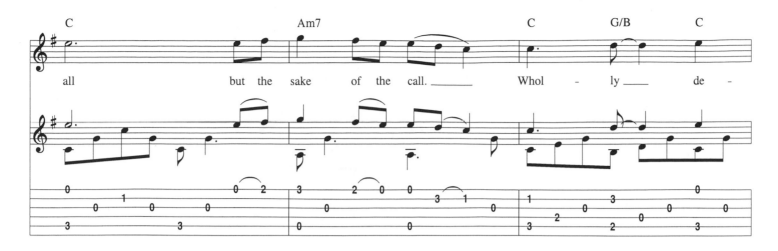

all but the sake of the call. _____ Whol - ly _____ de -

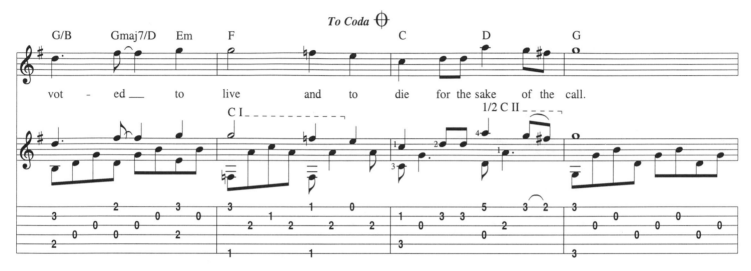

To Coda ⊕

vot - ed _____ to live and to die for the sake of the call.

D.S. al Coda
(take 2nd ending)

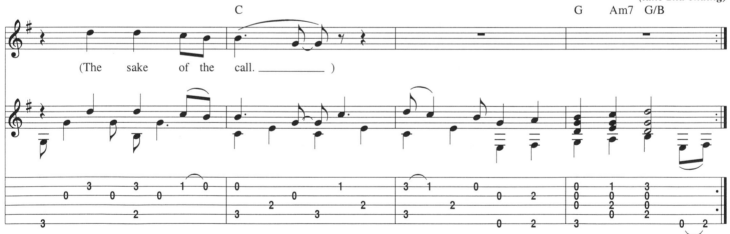

(The sake of the call. _____)

⊕ *Coda*

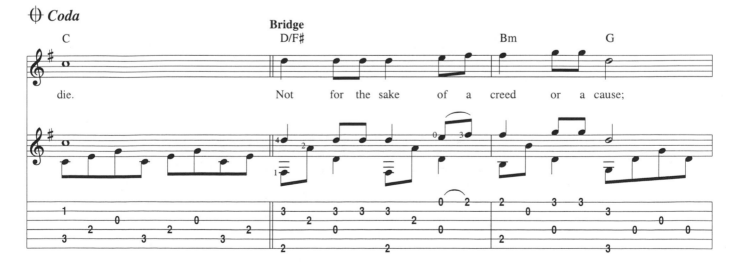

die. Not for the sake of a creed or a cause;

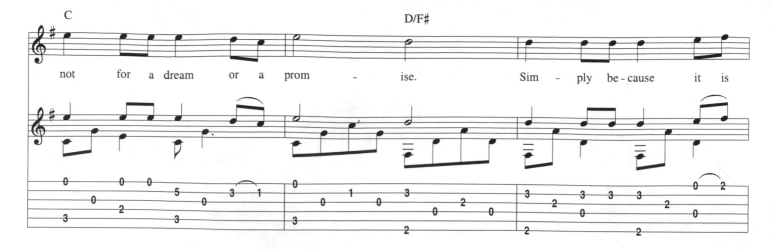

Outro-Chorus

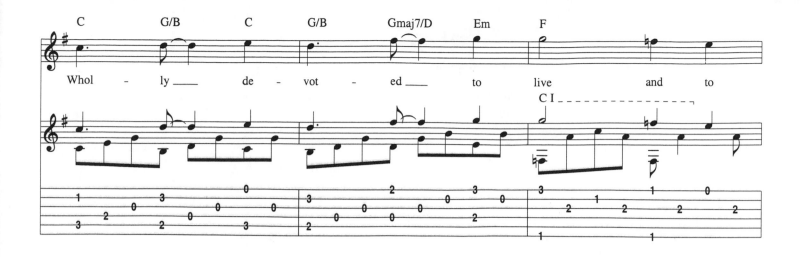

Whol - ly __ de - vot - ed __ to live and to

die for the sake of the call, for the sake of the

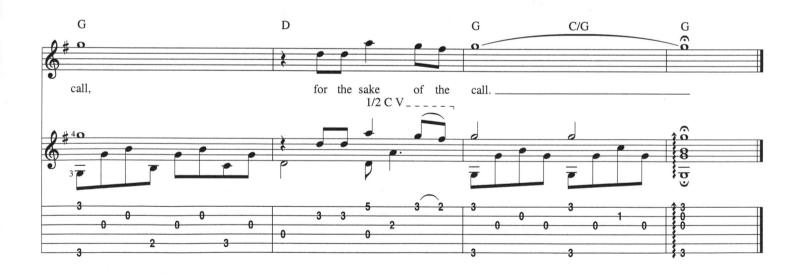

call, for the sake of the call. ___

Additional Lyrics

2. Empty nets lying there at the waters' edge.
   Told a story that few could believe
   And none could explain.
   How some crazy fishermen
   Agreed to go where Jesus lead,
   With no thought for what they would gain.
   Oh, Jesus had called them by name.
   And they answered:

3. Drawn like the rivers are drawn to the sea.
   There's no turnin' back
   For the water cannot help but flow.
   Once we hear the Savior's call
   We'll follow wherever He leads.
   Because of the love He has shown,
   And because He has called us to go,
   We will answer:

Busy Man

Words and Music by Steven Curtis Chapman

Drop D Tuning:
① = E ④ = D
② = B ⑤ = A
③ = G ⑥ = D

Intro
Moderately Fast

Oh, _____ here's a sto-ry 'bout a bus-y man. _____

Verse

1. I know _ a man named Bil-ly.
2. You've got a lot of nice things there, Bil-ly,

He's got al - most ev - 'ry - thing: _____
but they cost you more than you ___ know. _____

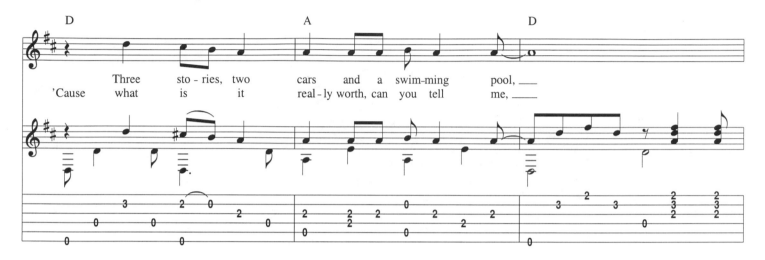

Three sto - ries, two cars and a swim-ming pool, ___
'Cause what is it real - ly worth, can you tell me, ___

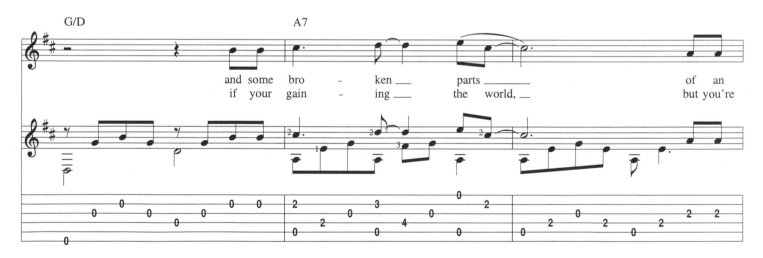

and some bro - ken ___ parts _____ of an
if your gain - ing ___ the world, ___ but you're

emp - ty ___ heart. _____ And I'm _____ think - in',
los - ing ___ your _____ soul? _____ And I'm think - in',

You're too bus-y man.

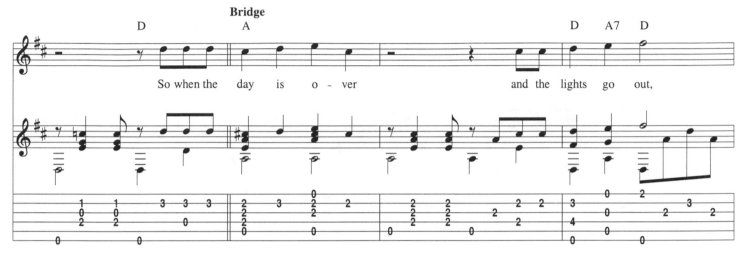

Bridge

So when the day is o - ver and the lights go out,

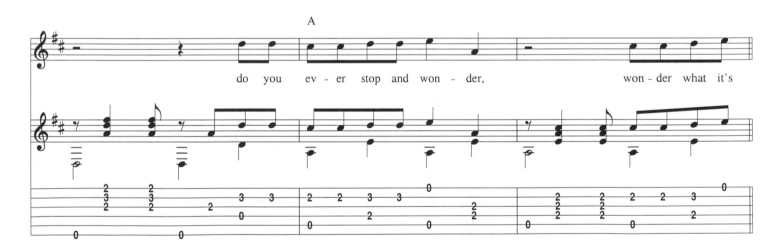

do you ev - er stop and won - der, won - der what it's

all a - bout, _____ won - der what it's all a - bout, _____
all a - bout? _____ You won - der what it's all a - bout. _____

D.S. al Coda

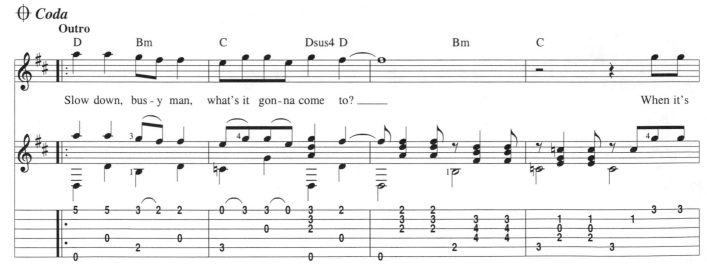

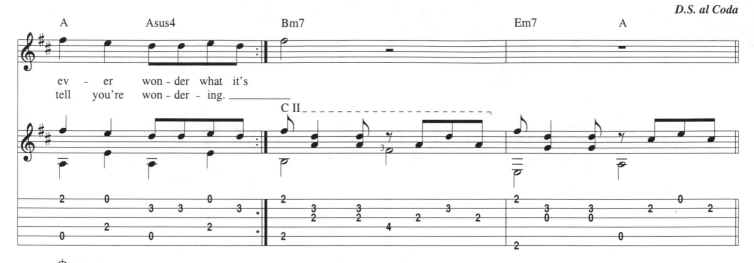

Heaven in the Real World

Words and Music by Steven Curtis Chapman

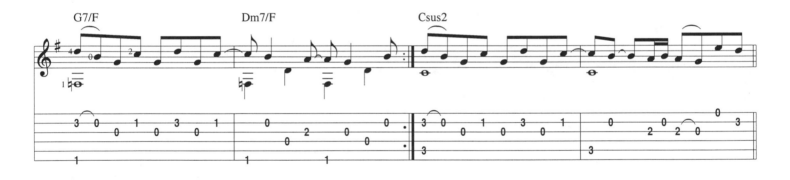

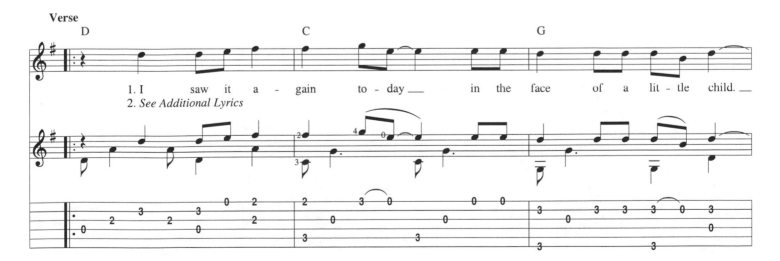

1. I saw it a - gain to - day __ in the face of a lit - tle child. __
2. *See Additional Lyrics*

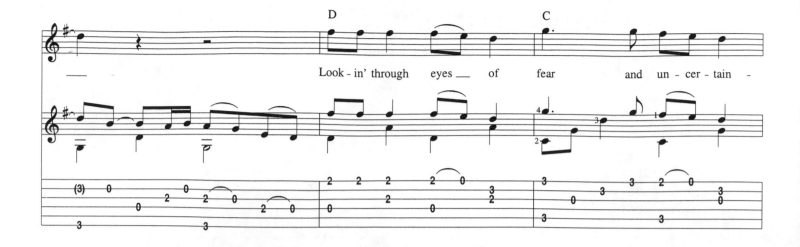

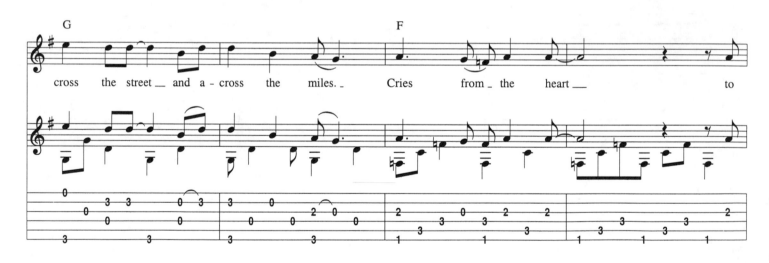

that will make ___ this life com - plete ___ for ev - 'ry man, _

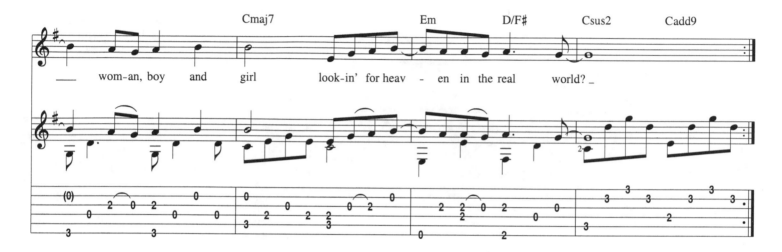

___ wom-an, boy and girl look-in' for heav - en in the real world? _

Bridge

Heav - en in the real world. It hap-pened one night ___ with a

ti - ny ba - by's birth _____ and God heard cre - a - tion cry - in'

and He sent heav - en to earth!

Outro

He is the hope, ___ he is the peace ___ that will

make this life com - plete. For ev - 'ry man, ___ wom - an, boy and girl look - in' for

heav - en in the real world. He is the peace that will make this life com -

plete,   for ev - 'ry man, ___ wom - an, boy   and   girl   look - in' for

heav-en in the real   world. ___   Heav-en has   come   to the real   world.

Additional Lyrics

2. To stand in the pourin' rain
   And believe the sun will shine again,
   To know that the grave is not the end;
   To feel the embrace of grace
   And cross the line where real life begins
   And know in your heart you've found the missing part.
   There is a hope, there is a peace
   That will make this life complete
   For ev'ry man, woman, boy and girl
   Lookin' for heaven in the real world.

The Great Adventure

Words and Music by Steven Curtis Chapman and Geoff Moore

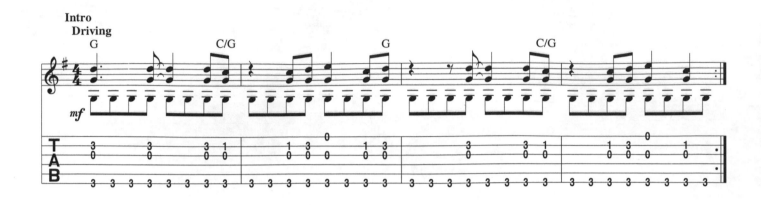

Start - ed out ___ this morn - ing in the u - su - al way, ___

chas - ing thoughts ___ in - side ___ my head ___ of all I

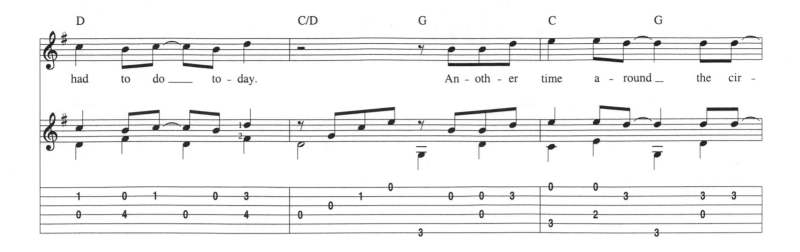

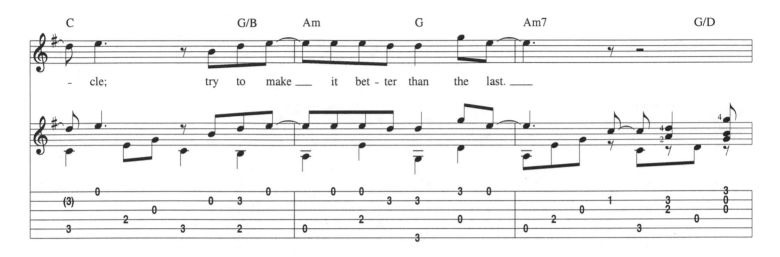

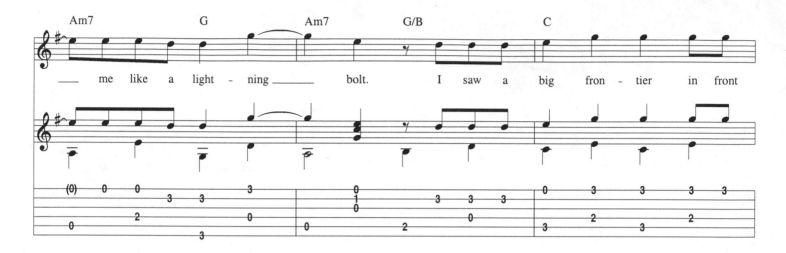

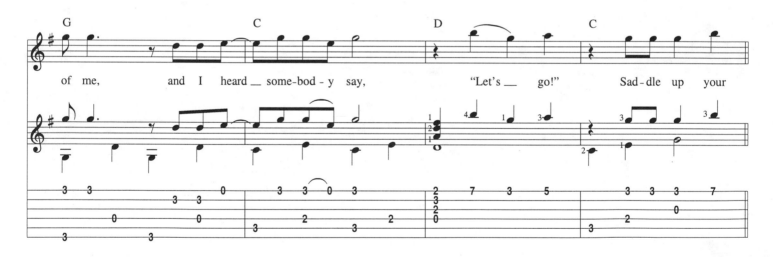

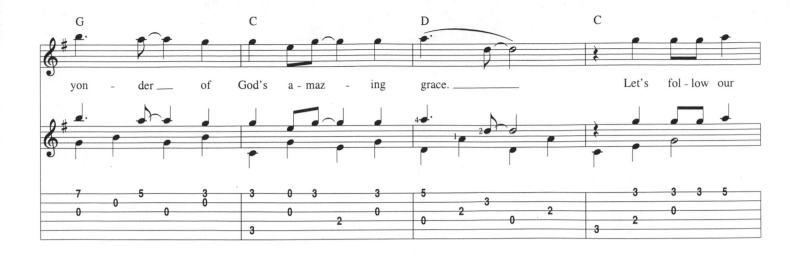

yon - der ___ of God's a - maz - ing grace. _____ Let's fol - low our

lead - er ___ in - to ___ the glo - ri - ous un - known. This is

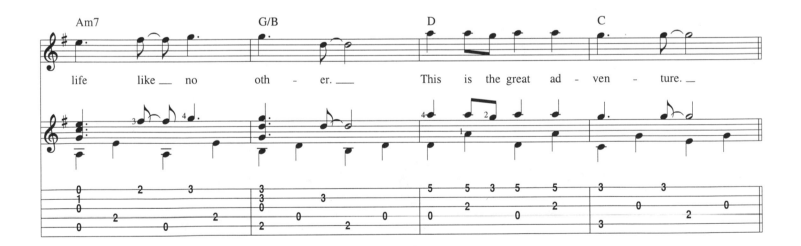

life like ___ no oth - er. ___ This is the great ad - ven - ture. ___

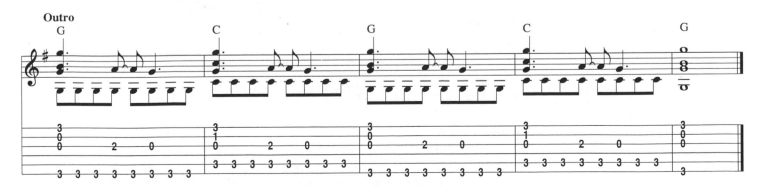

Outro

Hiding Place

Words and Music by Steven Curtis Chapman and Jerry Salley

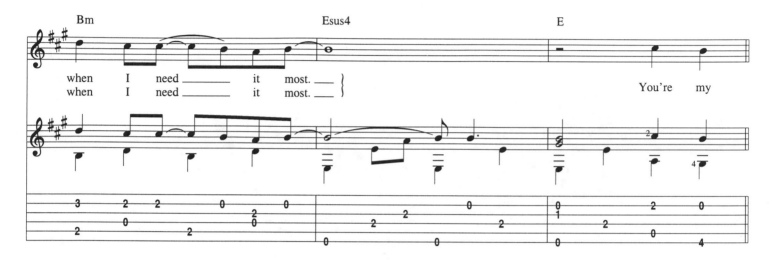

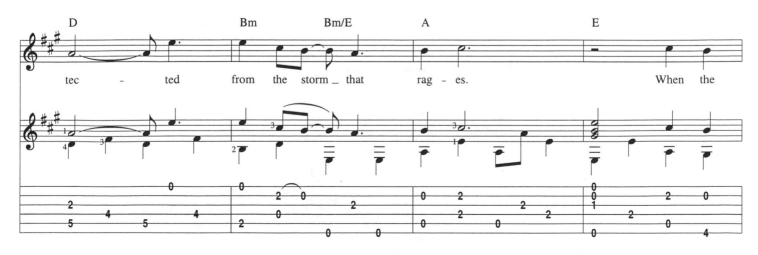

You're our on - ly ref - uge _____ when the rain comes pour - ing

down. _____ You're _ our _____

Chorus

hid - ing place. Safe in Your _____ em - brace we're pro -

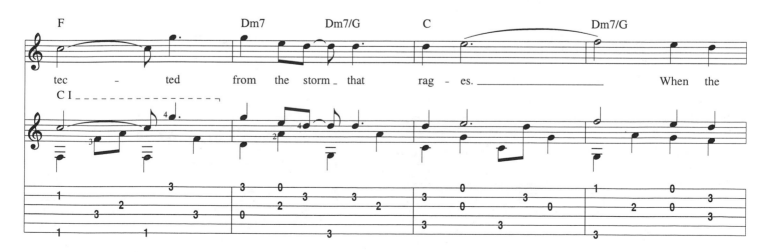

tec - ted from the storm _ that rag - es. _____ When the

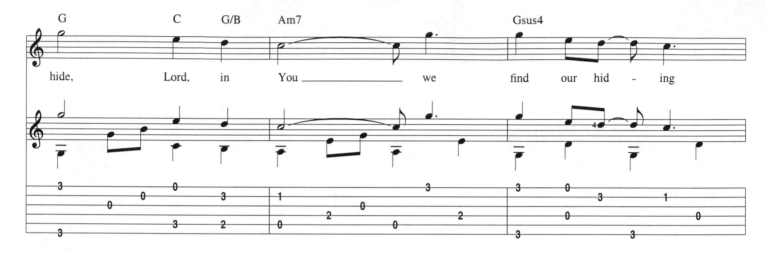

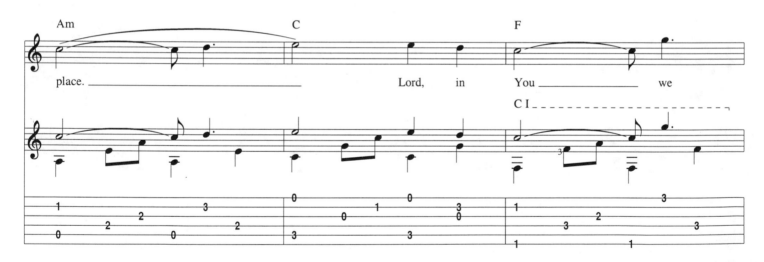

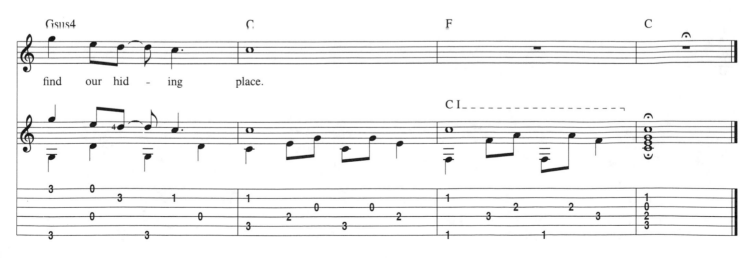

His Strength Is Perfect

Words and Music by Steven Curtis Chapman and Jerry Salley

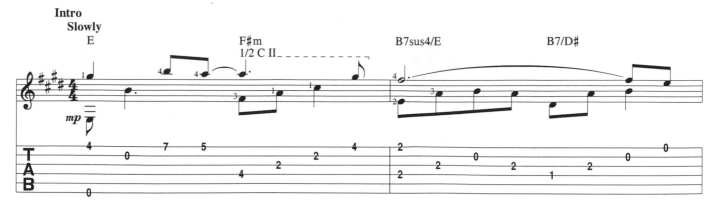

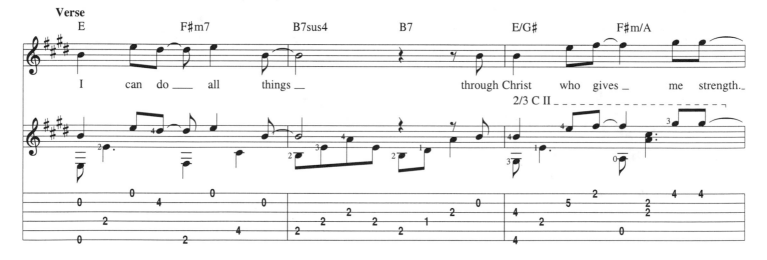

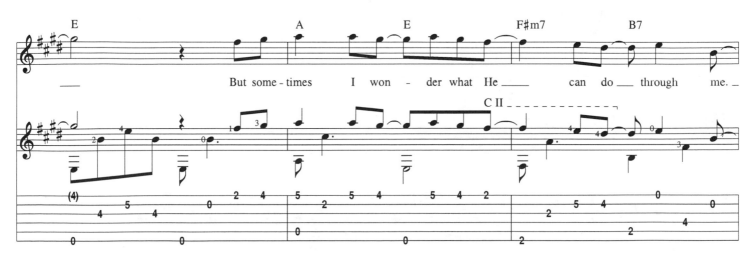

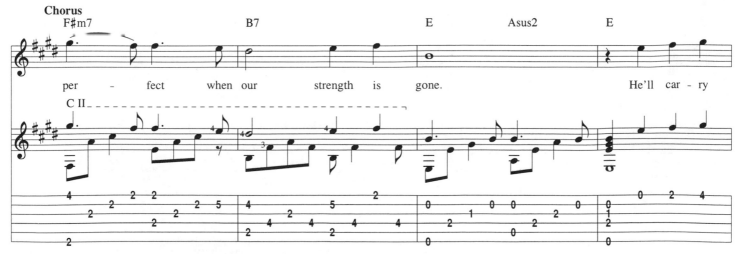

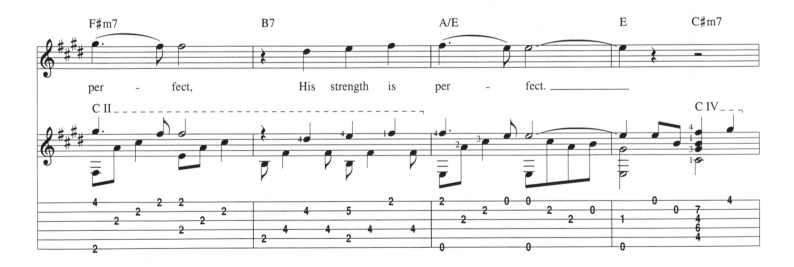

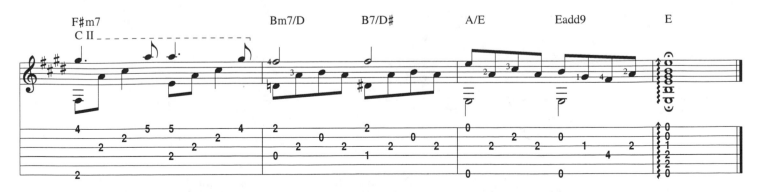

His Eyes

Words and Music by Steven Curtis Chapman and James Isaac Elliott

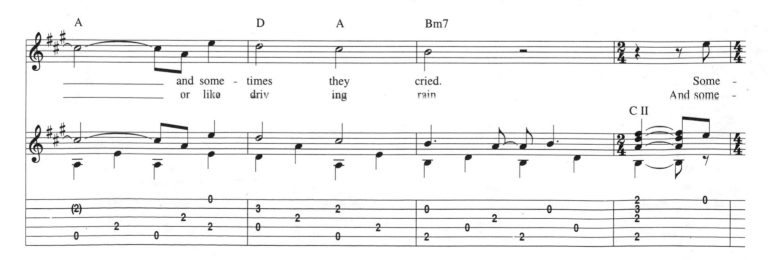

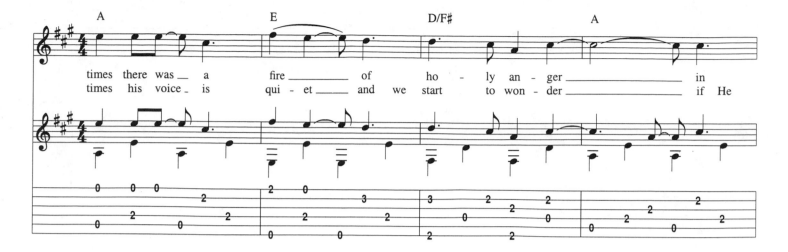

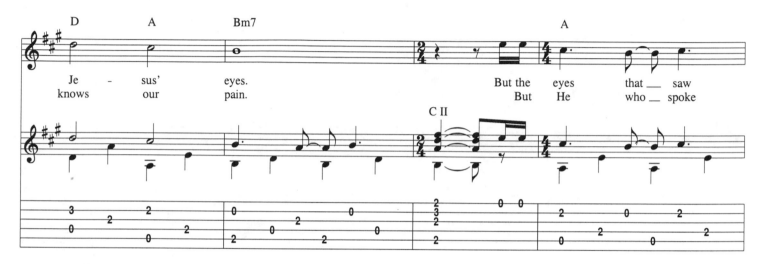

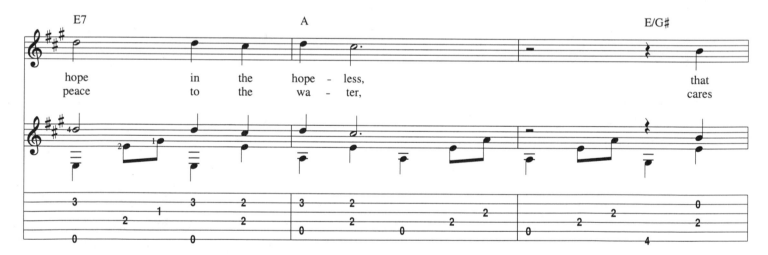

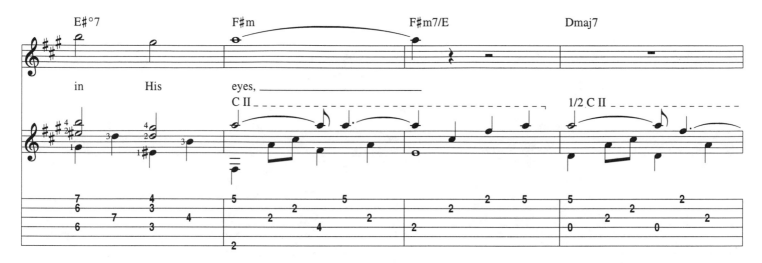

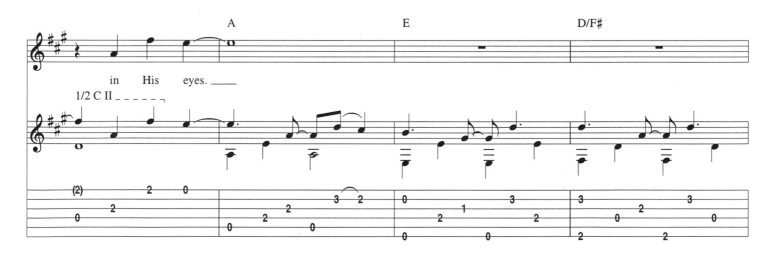

D.S. al Coda

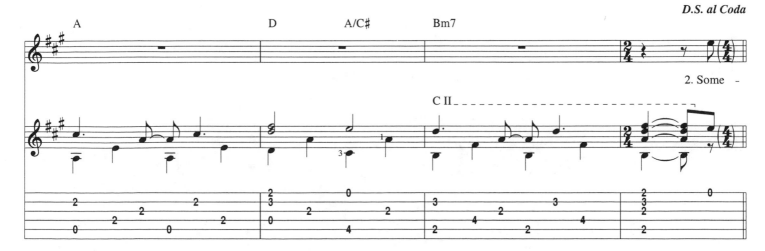

⊕ Coda

day, _____ to - day!   3. Some -

Verse

times I look ___ a - bove me _____ when stars are shin -

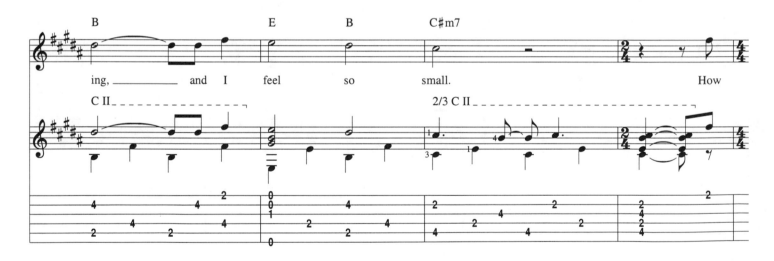

ing, _____ and I feel so small.   How

could the God __ of heav - en ____ and all cre - a - tion _____ know I'm

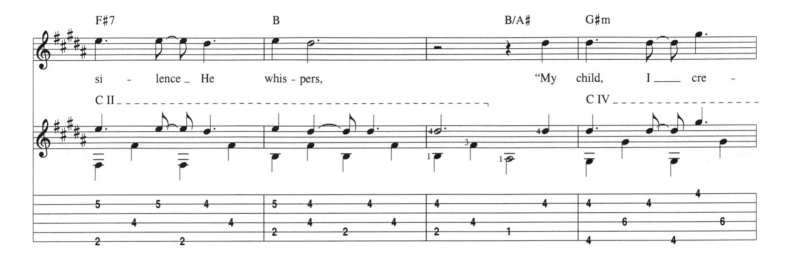

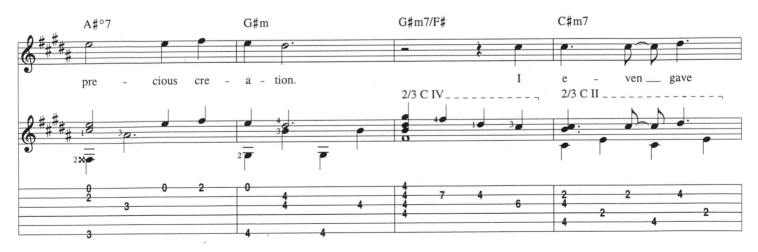

No mat - ter where you go, you __ will al - ways be __

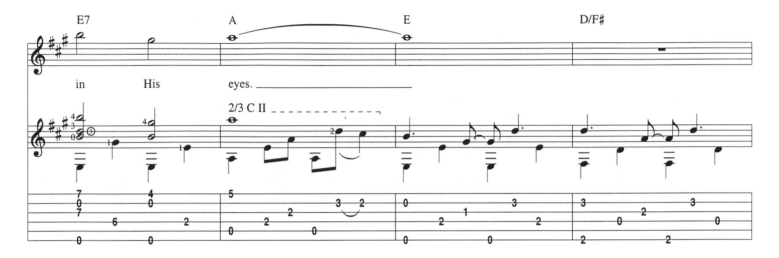

in His eyes. __

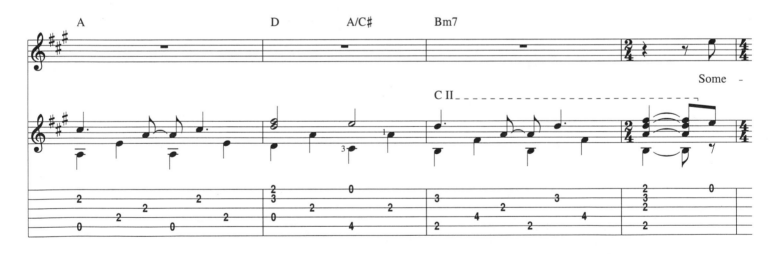

Some -

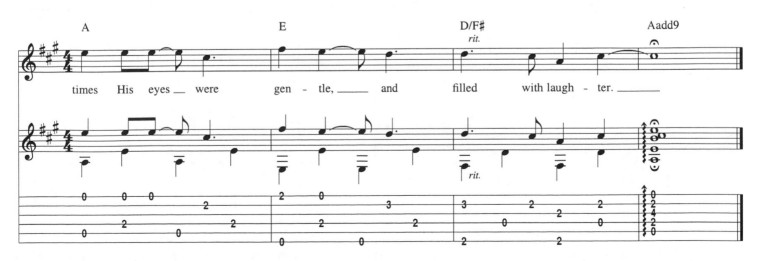

times His eyes __ were gen - tle, __ and filled with laugh - ter. __

More to This Life

Words and Music by Steven Curtis Chapman and Phil Naish

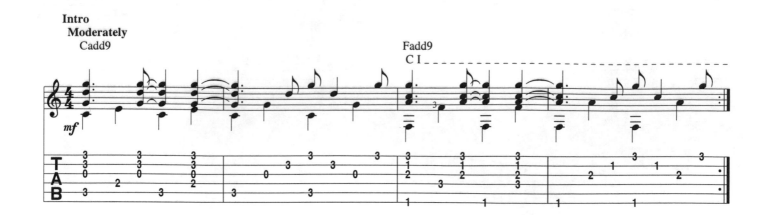

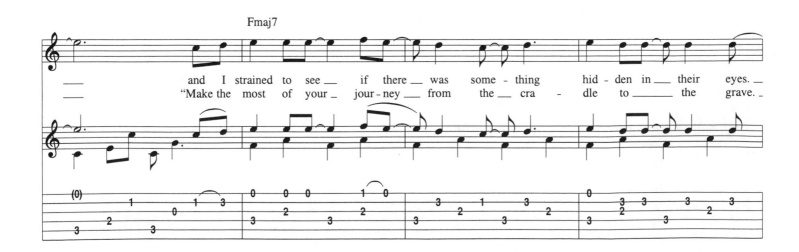

say,   "Life — just — goes   on."

day   life — must — go   on.

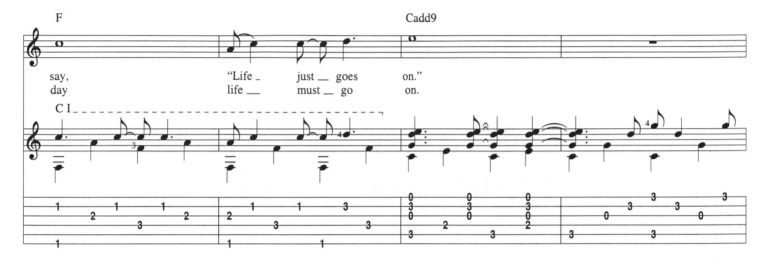

Chorus

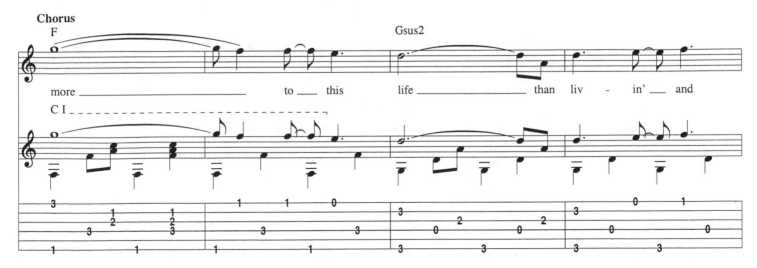

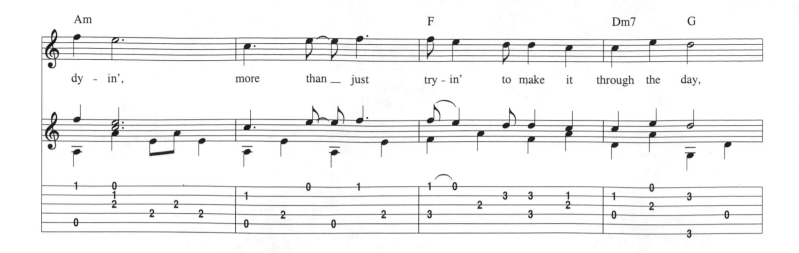

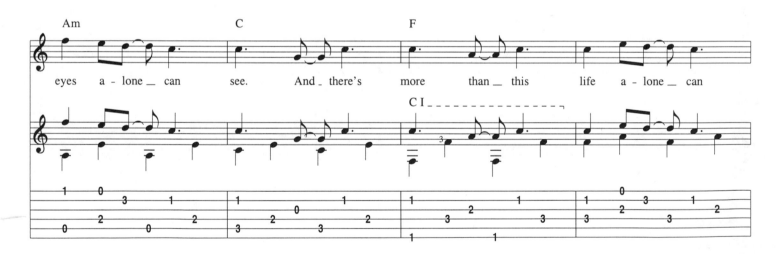

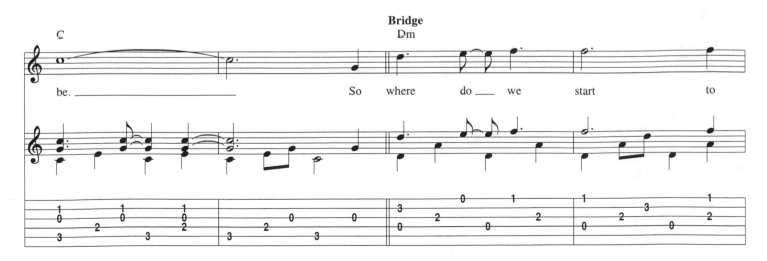

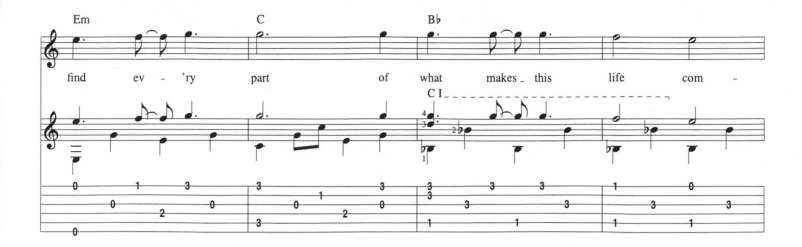

find ev - 'ry part of what makes _ this life com -

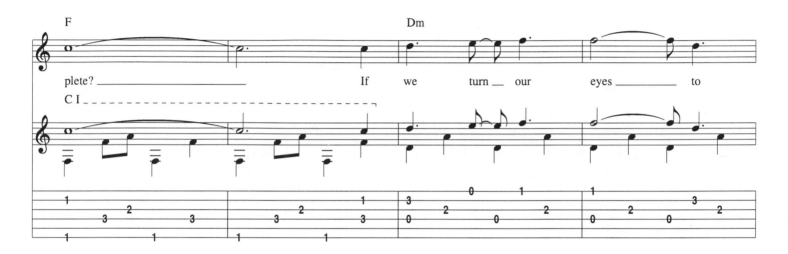

plete? _____ If we turn _ our eyes _____ to

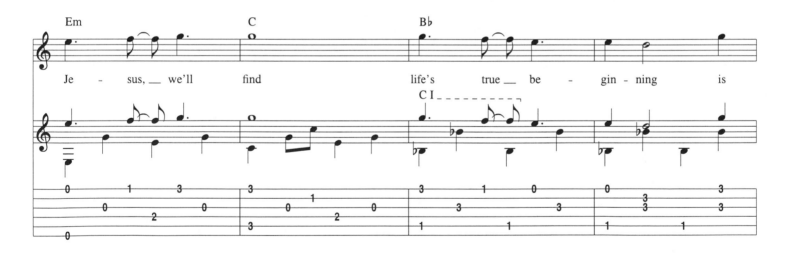

Je - sus, _ we'll find life's true _ be - gin - ning is

there at _ the cross where _ He died. To bring _ us

Outro-Chorus

more   to ___ this   life _____ than   liv - in' ___ and   dy - in'.

More   than ___ just   try - in'   to make   it   through the   day.   More   to ___ this

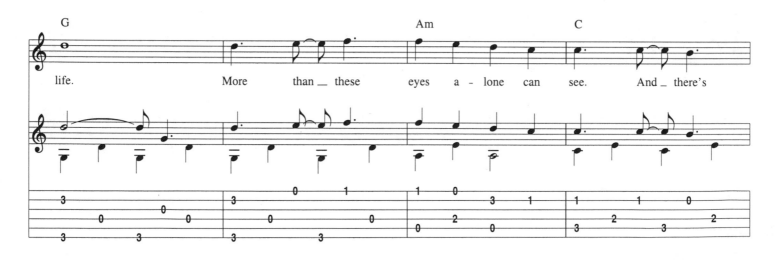

life.   More   than ___ these   eyes   a - lone   can   see.   And _ there's

more   to   this   life _____ than   liv - in' ___ and

44

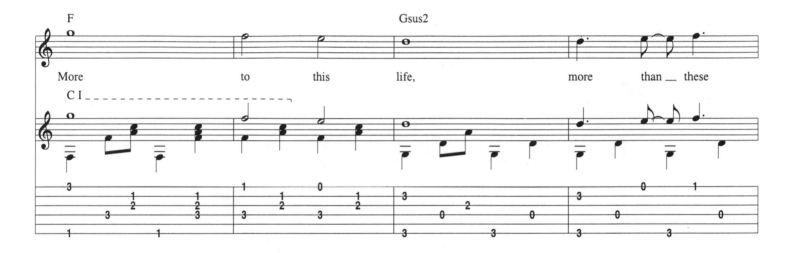

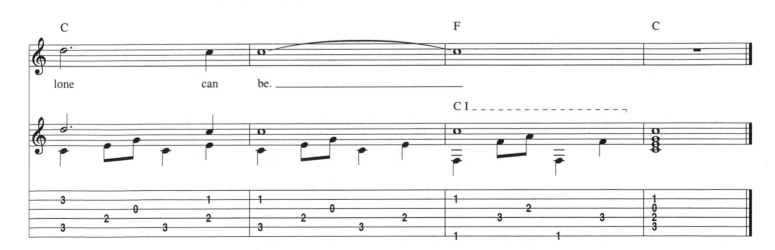

Hold on to Jesus

Words and Music by Steven Curtis Chapman and James Isaac Elliot

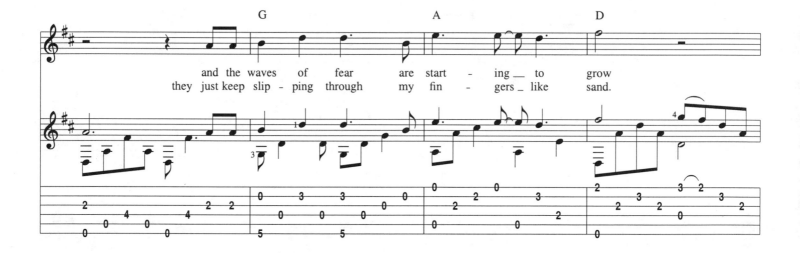

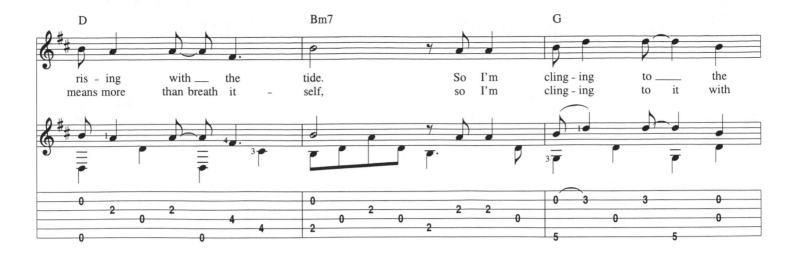

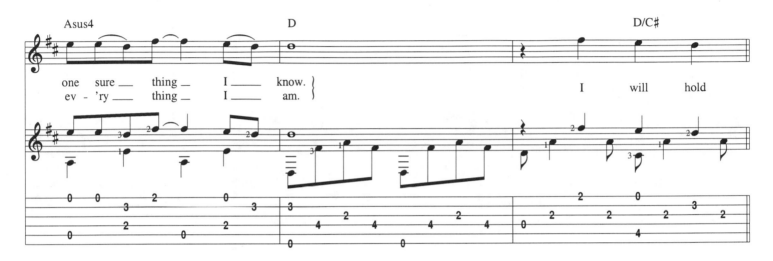

Chorus

loose - ly ____ to things that are fleet -

ing, and hold on ___ to Je-sus. I will hold _____ on to

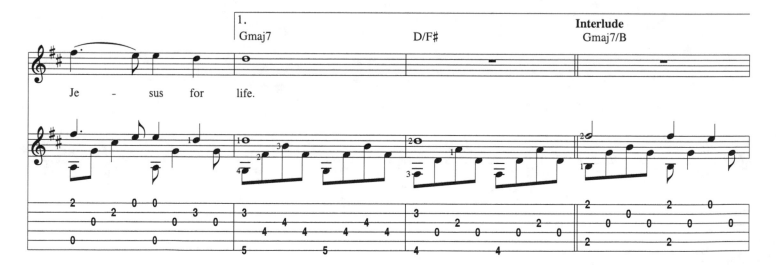

Je - sus for life.

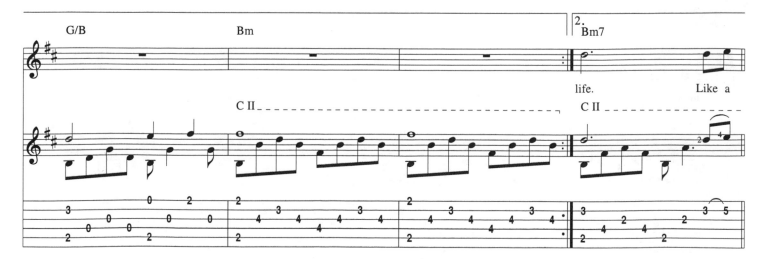

life. Like a

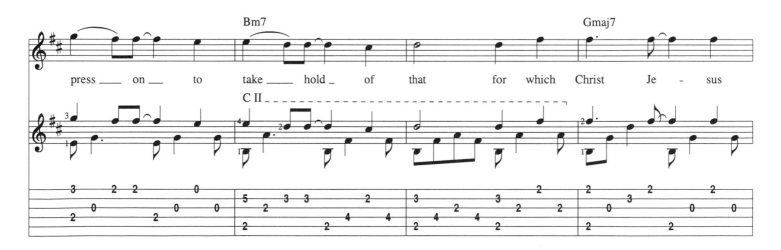

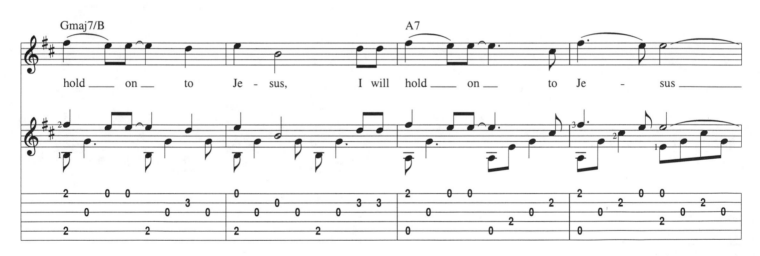

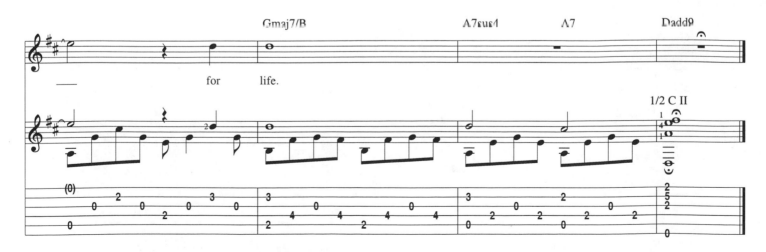

I Will Be Here

Words and Music by Steven Curtis Chapman

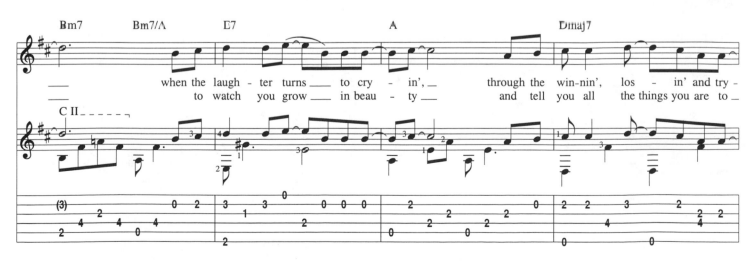

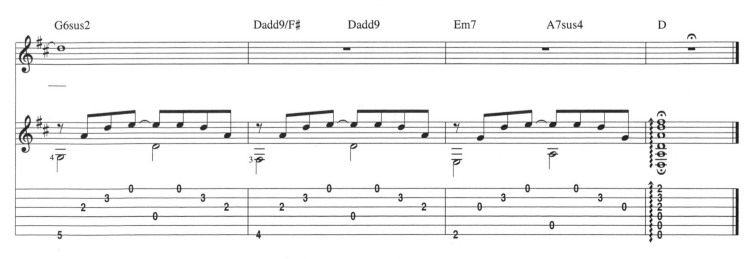

My Turn Now

Words and Music by Steven Curtis Chapman and Brent Lamb

Drop D Tuning:
① = E ④ = D
② = B ⑤ = A
③ = G ⑥ = D

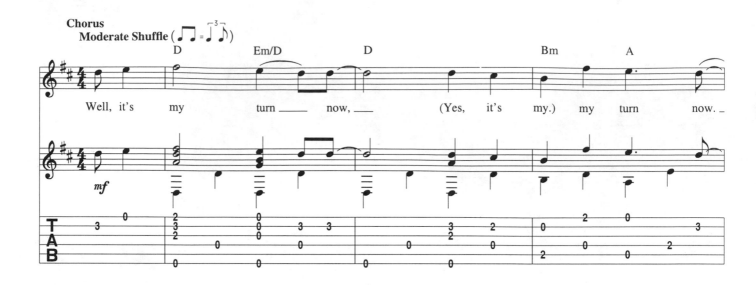

Verse

1., 2. I close the book and I shake my head. _____ Some-times I can't be-lieve the

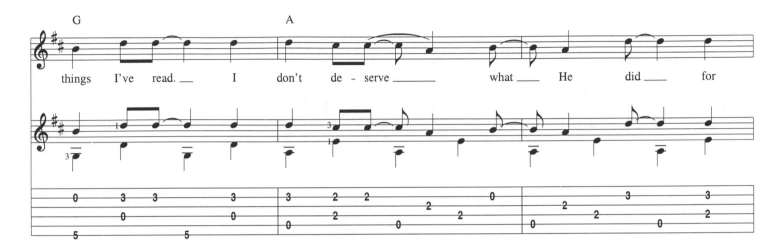

things I've read. _____ I don't de-serve _____ what _____ He did _____ for

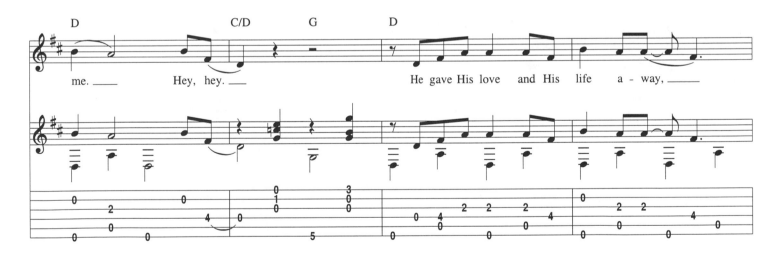

me. _____ Hey, hey. _____ He gave His love and His life a - way, _____

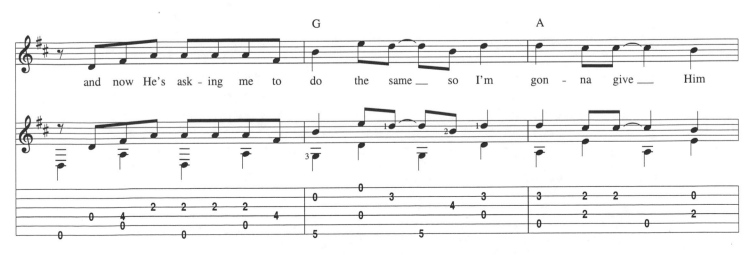

and now He's ask - ing me to do the same _____ so I'm gon - na give _____ Him

all I am, and all I ev - er hope to be. 'Cause it's

Chorus

my turn now. Well, it's my turn now,

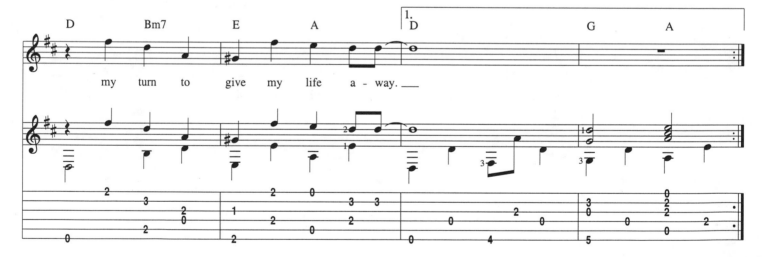

my turn to give my life a - way.

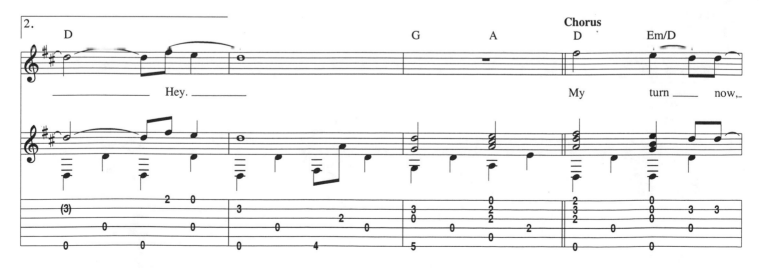

Hey. My turn now,

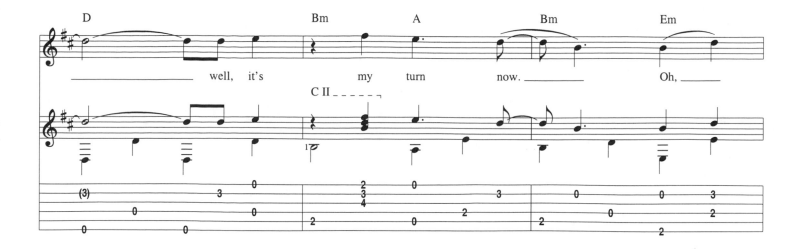

well, it's my turn now. Oh,

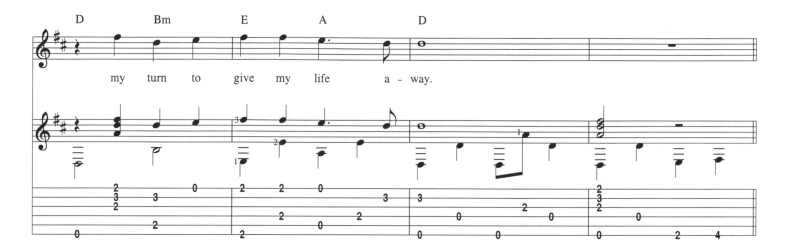

my turn to give my life a - way.

Bridge

My turn to say, "I love Him." My turn to let

Him know my life is His. So where He

57

Outro-Chorus

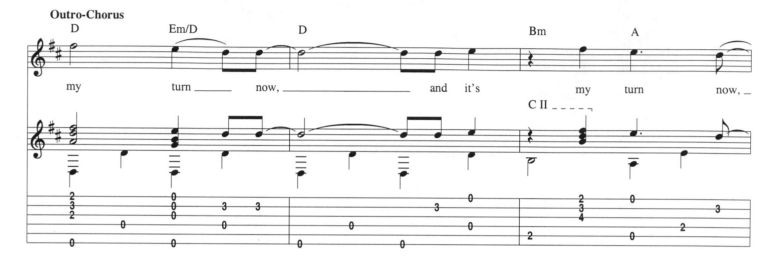

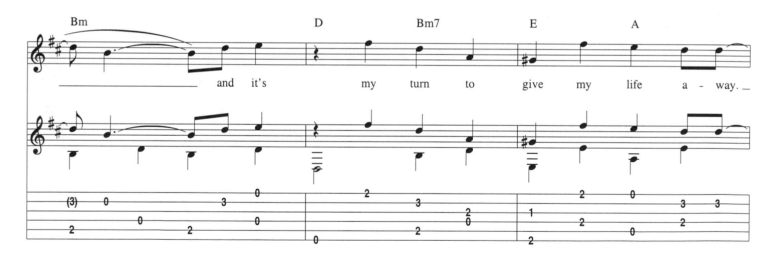

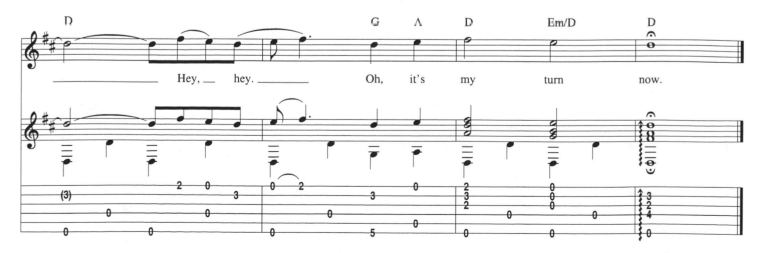

What Would I Say

Words and Music by Steven Curtis Chapman

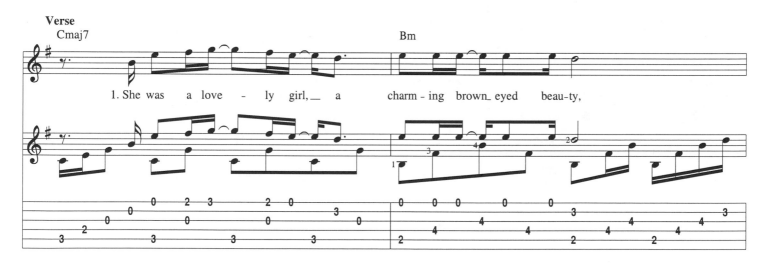

1. She was a love-ly girl,___ a charm-ing brown___ eyed beau-ty,

you were a bright ___ young man ___ who swept her off ___ her feet. ___

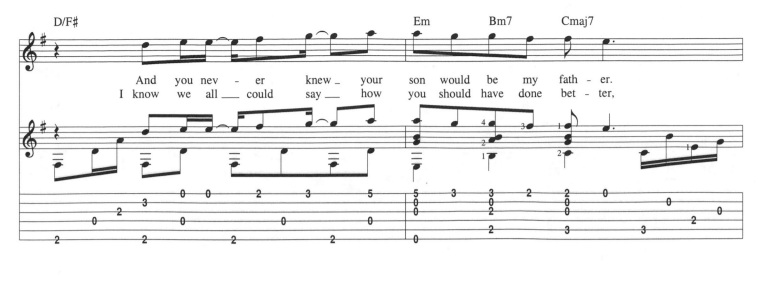

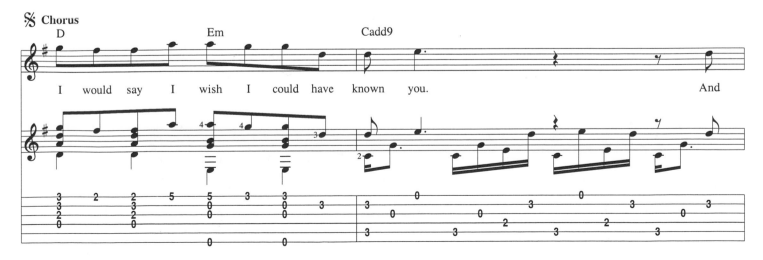

way your name's been car-ried.   These are things _I would   love to   tell you if __ I   could.   And

⊕ *Coda*

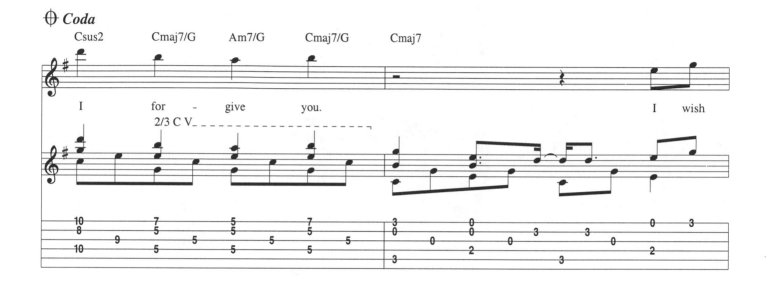

I   for - give   you.   I   wish

you   were   here   to   hear   what ___   I   would   say.

Outro

More Christian Music
for Guitar

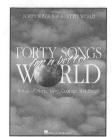

40 SONGS FOR A BETTER WORLD

40 songs with a message, including: All You Need Is Love • Bless the Beasts and Children • Colors of the Wind • Everything Is Beautiful • He Ain't Heavy...He's My Brother • I Am Your Child • Love Can Build a Bridge • What a Wonderful World • What the World Needs Now Is Love • You've Got a Friend • and more.

00702068 Easy Guitar with Notes & Tab.............$10.95

THE BEST OF STEVEN CURTIS CHAPMAN FOR EASY GUITAR

15 songs including: The Great Adventure • Heaven in the Real World • His Strength Is Perfect • I Will Be There • Move to This Life.

00702033 Easy Guitar with Notes & Tab.............$12.95

STEVEN CURTIS CHAPMAN FAVORITES

14 songs, including: Don't Let the Fire Die • Go There With You • Lord of the Dance • Runaway • When You Are a Soldier • and more.

00702073 Easy Guitar with Notes & Tab................$9.95

THE STEVEN CURTIS CHAPMAN GUITAR COLLECTION

12 of his most popular songs transcribed note-for-note for guitar, including: For the Sake of the Call • The Great Adventure • Heaven in the Real World • His Eyes • I Will Be Here • Lord of the Dance • More to This Life • Signs of Life • and more.

00690293 Guitar Transcriptions.........................$19.95

DC TALK – JESUS FREAK

Matching folio to this contemporary Christian band's crossover album. Songs include: Between You and Me • Jesus Freak • In the Light • Colored People • and more. Also includes photos.

00690184 Guitar Transcriptions..........................$19.95

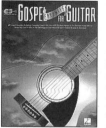

CONTEMPORARY CHRISTIAN FAVORITES

20 great easy guitar arrangements of contemporary Christian songs, including: El Shaddai • Friends • He Is Able • I Will Be Here • In the Name of the Lord • In Christ Alone • Love in Any Language • Open My Heart • Say the Name • Thy Word • Via Dolorosa • and more.

00702006 Easy Guitar with Notes & Tab................$9.95

FAVORITE HYMNS FOR EASY GUITAR

48 hymns, including: All Hail the Power of Jesus' Name • Amazing Grace • Be Thou My Vision • Blessed Assurance • Fairest Lord Jesus • I Love to Tell the Story • In the Garden • Let Us Break Bread Together • Rock of Ages • Were You There? • When I Survey the Wondrous Cross • and more.

00702041 Easy Guitar with Notes & Tab................$9.95

GOSPEL FAVORITES FOR GUITAR

An amazing collection of 50 favorites, including: Amazing Grace • Did You Stop to Pray This Morning • He Lives • His Name Is Wonderful • How Great Thou Art • The King Is Coming • My God Is Real • Nearer, My God, To Thee • The Old Rugged Cross • Take My Hand, Precious Lord • Turn Your Radio On • Will the Circle Be Unbroken • and more.

00699374 Easy Guitar with Notes & Tab.............$14.95

BEST OF AMY GRANT

18 of her best arranged for easy guitar, including: Angels • Baby Baby • Big Yellow Taxi • Doubly Good to You • El Shaddai • Every Heartbeat • Find a Way • Good for Me • House of Love • Lead Me On • Lucky One • Tennessee Christmas • and more.

00702099 Easy Guitar with Notes & Tab...............$9.95

GREATEST HYMNS FOR GUITAR

48 hymns, including: Abide With Me • Amazing Grace • Be Still My Soul • Glory to His Name • In the Garden • and more.

00702116 Easy Guitar with Notes & Tab...............$7.95

MAKING SOME NOISE – TODAY'S MODERN CHRISTIAN ROCK

13 songs, including: Big House • Cup • Flood • God • Jesus Freak • Shine • Soulbait • and more.

00690216 Guitar Transcriptions.........................$14.95

TODAY'S CHRISTIAN FAVORITES

19 songs, including: Daystar • Find Us Faithful • Go West Young Man • God and God Alone • He Is Exalted • I Will Choose Christ • Jubilate • My Turn Now • A Perfect Heart • Revive Us, O Lord • and more.

00702042 Easy Guitar with Notes & Tab...............$8.95

FOR MORE INFORMATION, SEE YOUR LOCAL MUSIC DEALER, OR WRITE TO:

HAL•LEONARD® CORPORATION

7777 W. BLUEMOUND RD. P.O. BOX 13819 MILWAUKEE, WI 53213

Prices, contents and availability subject to change without notice.
Some products may not be available outside the U.S.A.